**salmon**poetry

The

# TRUTH

### & Other Stories

# Sarah Clancy

**salmon**poetry

Published in 2014 by
Salmon Poetry
Cliffs of Moher, County Clare, Ireland
Website: www.salmonpoetry.com
Email: info@salmonpoetry.com

ISBN 978-1-908836-91-5

COVER IMAGE: Sarah Clancy
COVER DESIGN & TYPESETTING: *Siobhán Hutson*
*Printed in Ireland by Sprint Print*

*Salmon Poetry gratefully acknowledges the support of*
*The Arts Council / An Chomhairle Ealaoín*

*The study of dreams is particularly difficult, for we cannot examine dreams directly, we can only speak of the memory of dreams. And it is possible that the memory of dreams does not correspond directly to the dreams themselves.*

JORGE LUIS BORGES
from 'Nightmares' in *Seven Nights* (1977)

*The person who distrusts himself has no touchstone for reality – for this touchstone can only be oneself. Such a person interposes between himself and reality nothing less than a labyrinth of attitudes. And these attitudes, furthermore, though the person is usually unaware of it (is unaware of so much!), are historical and public attitudes.*

JAMES BALDWIN
from *The Fire Next Time* (1962)

# Acknowledgments

Thanks to the editors of the following publications in which some of these poems first appeared: *The Stinging Fly, The Poetry Bus, Irish Left Review, The Moth, New Planet Cabaret, The Penny Dreadful, Skylight 47, Penduline* (USA), *OFI Press* (Mexico), *Poetry 24*, Doire Press's *North Beach Nights Anthology Two, Bare Hands, The Galway Review, What's the Story* (USA), *Poethead* and *Numero Cinq* (Canada).

Thanks to Megan Buckley, Elaine Feeney, Rita Ann Higgins, Martin Dyar, Aoibheann Mc Cann, Katherine O'Donnell and Dani Gill who all read and commented on various drafts of this manuscript, to Dave Lordan, Declan Meade, Stephen Murray, Kevin Higgins, Susan Millar Du Mars, Stephen James Smith, John Walsh and Lisa Frank for encouragement and a whole variety of opportunities that wouldn't have come about without them, to Judith Mok and Michael O'Loughlin who sent me to the side of a wild cliff in Kerry in the month of February, to James Harrold for his support, to Paul Garrett and Vicky Donnelly for dogged persistent friendship and some brilliant observations which I pilfered, to Maria Mc Manus for being the one on the spot, to the late Seamus Heaney whose poems 'Postcript' and 'Digging' somehow sneaked their way into two of the poems in this collection, and to all the editors, festival organisers, embassy staff, radio presenters and encouraging people without whom writing poetry would be possible but more difficult and much less fun.

Super-extra thanks to Jessie and Siobhán at Salmon Poetry for all they've done and all they do.

*in appreciation of all my wonderful friends*
*but in particular and special memory of*

Kevin O'Shea

*a gentleman and a gentle man*

# Cold Cases

Some doors should stay shut
not all are portals
some conceal sleeping things
that are less ferocious
left undisturbed behind them,
let's whisper this time can't we?
Let's not go in there
sharp-stick-poking
turn now with me – this time
let's keep on walking.

# Contents

# Pagan's Votive

I pray for a poem without place names
for dislocation, for an end
to my mind's petty nationalisms
I pray for this harsh religion's downfall
for open-ended sentences
words with space in them
like limestone pavements
I pray for amulets in verses
that I can brandish against darkness
I pray that I will write
a disassociated poem that floats me with it
to somewhere without bitterness
I pray that I will wear it
like a scapular against cynicism
and that it will act as agent
to distil my anger into action
I pray that on pet days like this one
that somehow find me
in the sanctuary of St Bridget's well
beside a young person grieving
that it will make me able
that it will make me gentle.

# Dot Dot Dot

… for the striving, for the starlings all fetched up by cold
for the crow and his shriekery, for the everyday ebb
and its thievery, for the lap-dancing punters who look
into the faces of the prey they exploit, for the do-gooders
who wouldn't, the god-be-with-yous and for the dot the dot the dot

give me the freaks and the gimps and the soulless, the soupers
the jumpers, the lonely, give me incantations, give me formless
gaping lusts, grist for forlorn mills, give me three of a supposed
hundred sit ups, give me grievances – throw shadow, spread it, hurl it
in street corner doorways, stow it, sow it, reap questions with no answers

plant them grow them, pontificators, fornicators, give me
your seven-year itches, give me pictures and evocations, give me
devoutness and abstention offer up those paltry rusting incantations,
share loose beating ends, rough edges, unfurl allegiances and hang them
mock them, damn them, ticking streets crave your flat step, floorboards
your soft soles; roll up roll up roll up – we have plenty…

# Hair's Breadth

I sometimes keep an eye on you while your flat-screen television
projects flickering shadows along the garden wall at dusk
and I wonder why you never close the curtains.
Your dog knows me but he's old now and idle
you probably think he's dreaming when his stub tail thumps
the floorboards and his ears prick at the sound of my feet
crunching on your gravel path, but I know he's wondering
if I'll come in and feed him some more of the chocolate
he's not usually given, he's easily paid off that dog is –
one thin bar of Dairy Milk is all it took, the type some people
were offered in childhood by adults who wanted to groom them.

For devilment I sometimes scrape a twig across your window
and watch your senses kick in, you look around, and maybe
turn the sound down but then you settle, it's funny isn't it
how instinct doesn't leave us even when we no longer need it?
Some night when I'm leaving I'm going to ring the door bell,
well, that's what I tell myself, that's all, I tell myself,
I am under control, I will go to your door but I will not open it.

# Memory, Freud and the Detective Inspector

There was no water there.

You say there was no water.
Was it summer when this happened?

Yes.

Was it hot and were you there?

I don't remember.
I remember blue billed ducks and how they disappeared in water.

But you said there was no water.

No I said there was none there. I remember there was no water.

This is a simple matter.
Was it summer, were you hot and was there or was there not water?

The water I remember wasn't the same water that wasn't there.

# Selfie

There can be no poems on mornings like this
neither before nor after breakfast:
they've build a fake refugee camp at Davos
complete with soldiers and mock corpses
so the rich can dirty their shoe soles
can rough up their retinas in it
and then call it experience
world leaders can lean in to conflict zone chic
and lecture us afterwards on how we can,
should and must flourish in adversity –
sure didn't they visit
a very close simulation of it?

My radio is spewing indistinguishable headlines
of how everything everywhere is better
and the rain is relentless, streets here are sleazy from it
and parents drive steam-filled cars full
of their sugar-filled offspring past my windows
they're sending them off to learn
to be simulations of obedient citizens
and my bed is a pit of insomnia, in this country
where people of conscience are jailed
the self won't stand up to questioning
it can't bear interrogations like this
the self won't get up out of bed today
and I can't say I blame it.

# And Yet We Must Live In These Times

*for Paul M. Garrett who saw the signs*

In at the housing office the woman says
if I need a house then I'll have to tell the council
I'm homeless or else bunk in with my parents
and I feel the heat of tears in my eyes and let me tell you
it's not sadness I'm feeling, it's anger;
after all of my years insisting that no one
will ever call me victim, in they come
and do it from a whole different angle
I didn't see coming
and they call it helping –
these are the times that I live in
still paying the tail end of my mortgage
with no home to show for it
and I wonder what I've absorbed that means
even with all of my theories, my politics
this, the oldest human endeavour
of seeking out shelter
has become shame-filled
and on my way down through town
Rosali asks for a fiver. I give it
it's easier to offer than to ask, I reckon
she says 'You are beautiful' showing the limits
of her English vocabulary but I'm not,
what I am is damaged and raging –
on days like this I seek the sea out and breathe it
and you, what do you do to get through it?

Don't call it apathy, we're not fine
we're not grand, thanks, we are hurt
and we're making it worse by pretending we're sorted.
I walk past Griffin's Bakery as if I am the only one
in this river of people on Shop Street
who's rocking a sub-plot
who's got things going on
in the background that take effort to deal with

and that's why it's called individualism isn't it?
Because we aren't telling anyone
in the separation of one from each other
of ourselves from ourselves
we're alienated, but sure it's grand isn't it?
We're on the pig's back
and yet we must live in these times,

and I write down past tense love affairs
all the while getting older and worn out
and what use is it? Resuscitating old lovers
for nothing recycling these slogans, these dictums
if I can't write about real things why bother?
If I can't mock the signs on the wall in Welfare
that say after two decades of working
I'm likely to drink in the daytime
to have poor personal hygiene,
or to spit and swear at the people who work there
and are only paying their bills same as anyone.

I fool myself that one of these days I might do it
might hurt someone, wreck something
and it might bring me to some other dimension
that's human so they tell me, competition
and viciousness but I say that's fiction
I reassure you that I won't let it happen
the truth is, I don't have it in me
I'm lacking some cruelty

because I think what's human is order and interdependence
what's human is balance and kindness and humour
and us coming up with a way we can live
in these times without violence,
we must live in these times and no other.

I, for one, might need some help with it
is that too much to ask for?

# Doppelgänger

In Clew Bay's shallows chewed-up lumps of islands loiter
with one-storey dwellings clinging to their deformed edges
like adolescents on street corners, not one thing is regular
and I won't ask who lives here or who in this wasteland cares.
The tide is so high that it's impossible to walk to the houses without
wading waist-deep in the detritus of this absolutely smalltime coastline
but not far enough in to refloat a flatlining boat. It's abandoned
face down at the shoreline, left there, like me, stranded
in this ugly mud and sand land that can only dream of pasture.
Oh it's long past listing that dingy is beached, bereft of any dignity
and I am strung out. Collie dog cocks his leg and pees on it
and I'm long past listening to those Brent geese getting
the hell out of here, the whirs and hoots of them escape me
because I'm exposed here. I'm mainlining electricity from overhead wires
shhh, listen! They are singing-howling-whistling down in my gut
and out through the greyness of this autumn dusk. Their twang
could be from Siberia but on my hairline the wires burn
a thin cold bellow and I like it, I like the winsome collie dog
and the streaks of sea water rust on his white brisket, how it seeps
from his clammed-up collar-buckle as he brings me the same piece
of sea-jaded timber over and over and over and I am on the air now
whinnying, I'm twanging like a string plucked and echoing,
here I am my own doppelganger. I am listening.
Can you hear me listening and don't I sound just like myself?

# Industrialist

*for Katherine*

Often on clear nights she stands on the overpass watching car lights
disappear in the distance and she waits for the smell of food frying
in the bright kitchens beneath her, to make way for exhaust fumes
which she inhales deeply as if they could fuel her.

She loves illuminated toll booths and the flow of cars through them,
they give her the shivers in ways she doesn't know how to explain
she's besotted with flyovers, with underground car parks and empty
office buildings with their rows and rows of blank windows.

She'd like to stroke the rusting arcs of the ship prows lined up
in the harbour before they weigh anchor and if she could she'd kit out
her whole life with rivets and practical checker-plate metal
and the patterns that diesel spills make on still water surfaces.

She loves uneven heaps of scrap metal and the trademarks
on shipping containers stacked down at the dockyards –
the thought of all that lucky merchandise being transported
to other places almost, but not quite, takes her with it.

# Someone's Always Losing Someone Else

*for Lisa, Anna and Nicky*

*– Train Wreck*
The last time you missed me
was with a rock at my window
and the last time I missed you
was when I had that book
I wanted to give you but
then I didn't because you'd got that dog then,
and you looked contented.
Believe it or not I think
I might have been jealous of it
but I told myself, going on precedent,
there's a good chance we'll just wreck this
so I left it and at Christmas you texted
saying I miss you already
and I said what is it with us? What is it?
And you just sent xxxs.
We were a train wreck
and I already miss you.

*– I Want you Back*
And I'll remember Cuba Nightclub,
you dancing to the Jackson Five
and us fizzing out into Eyre Square later
with you telling me no day-trippers need apply,
not some Month's Mind notice
on a shop window in the rain, years later
insisting that you've died.

*– Bell, Book and Candle*
You'll open the slim book you bought for two euros
in the secondhand shop: Sartre, what else?
On its title page you'll find
your friend's name written in blue ink,
it's a small town this one, the smallest,
you'll flick through it to the page
where she's got the words *anguish*
*abandonment* and *despair* underlined in red
and you'll find you've nothing left to say.

*– Meanwhile*
You'll stop in front of the pharmacy
thinking of tranquilisers but knowing
the nerve endings that are holding you up
would give way in a clock tick if
you gave them the slightest excuse.
You won't let them. That's vital.
You'll go in though and sit
in the photo booth, you'll feed coins to it
and take what it offers:
four little squares with your face on them
proof, of some kind or another.
Proof your own flesh couldn't give you.

*– Lost Souls and Popcorn*
And I'll see boys who look like you
and you and you and me on screen
in stolen-afternoon cinema trips
where everyone's an orphan
where everyone's cast out and timeless
and I'll know at the outset there's no future in it
but I'll sit through it mouth open
and let my popcorn fall unnoticed
even though I know who did it and who didn't
I'll watch the credits 'till they're finished
I'll watch the credits 'till they're finished
I'll watch the credits 'till they're finished.

# Corral

I will build a post and rail corral
somewhere already sheltered
by old and patient trees.
One by one I'll bring you all there
to idle by the water trough
or graze in the old oak's shade.
I'll patrol the boundary fence
and when night comes
I'll sleep standing, one ear listening
for the would-be rustlers who
signal their intentions through the air.
I'll keep watch, I'll keep you safe
love is easier from here
than when we have to graze
      the same fields together.

# It's the Dark

*a poem for my selves*

On this day of halogen and helium
we are dodging shadows
our eyes squinting against late afternoon sun
but it's with us, despite the whiteness
it's a hand not held
in a dark bedroom, in a dark house, on a dark street
where no one ever thought to leave a light on for us
it's every unblown birthday candle
a school of sorts, an education,
it's a taunting lane with pine trees and a wind channelled down it,
it's the terror that made our fat legs pedal faster
made us flee it,
as if, in the bright lights of the kitchen hours later
we still wouldn't feel it
it's that car journey we didn't want to go on
those other headlights sweeping past in freedom
and our relentless windscreen wipers beating rhythm
to the place we swore we'd never get to
on a morning night wouldn't relinquish,
it's a bridge in an inferno crumbling
and I can tell you there's no crossing back over
it's the confessional where we don't know what to say
or even who to answer to,
it's a hundred pagan folk memories;
nameless, because they never tried to conquer it,
it's the dark
it's the dark
it's the dark
and it's best to leave it be.

# Square Peg

On pale grey days like this one when the smoke from early fires hung in
unaccustomed air, when autumn colours were still uniform and flat
I would have kept on walking out through the small town morning.

I would have stowed my schoolbag in a hedge, passed the school gates
slinking until I came to Shantalla where things got safer
for un-uniformed schoolday children.

I would have crossed the playing field behind the blue-jeans factory,
skirting abandoned traffic cones and the shopping trolley chariots
leftover from some half-delinquent game.

I would have headed uphill towards Rahoon where I could go
completely unremarked on except by two thin Lurchers
and a stub tailed Jack Russell, barking.

Hands in pockets I would have gone up to the reservoir and sat there
looking at the pattern of the city laid out below me and I'd have known
I had the run of it as far as my legs could cope with.

I would have gone up higher to the mast at Tóin na Brocaí
where I might have shared my sandwiches with some seagull's squawks
and plunges and the disembodied traffic noises.

Maybe I'd have looked down at the lake and watched miniature rowers
sending water lapping to its edges and scaring wildfowl skywards or
I could have walked along the river bank towards town, picking reeds
and splitting them before squeezing out their pulpy innards.

I would have stopped to whicker back at the heavy old pony
who kept gentle sentry at Dangan and always blew in greeting –
not at all surprised to see me, that's the thing about horses see,
they don't know where you should be.

I would have smoked discarded Carrolls cigarette butts
in Bunker Lydon's corrugated sheds with the smell and soft sounds
of cattle chewing wrapped around me like a blanket. I would have been
so far from chaos from the vulgar schoolyard yelling

that it would have seemed a whole other existence far beyond explaining
to the principal, or my parents when they brought me to his office
demanding to be told what it was I did when I was off school, mitching:

all I could ever say was 'nothing' taking still familiar refuge
in insolence for something I didn't understand myself, by now though
I know the only problem was that they were asking
the wrong person the wrong question.

# Gutted

Words desert me —
my lips are cracked and bitten
my stomach carved
its innards are delighting
in their own exposure
but I must not shout this
not me, I must move forwards
must walk on with
loose bones clanking
stiff joints creaking
I must forget enough
to drop from numb to earthling
I must back-track to some
all-you-can-eat buffet of suffering
some re-birthing

and now I wish my shoes
would hurt me
I wish for blisters
I wish for vinegar and mustard
some bitter alchemy
to send my blood corpuscles
surging, I wish once more
for my own bones broken
for a split lip, a shattered jaw
a thick ear, I wish
for something to fill this
absence, something
to keep my brazen guts in.

# My Thoughts Are Carrots
# My Thoughts Are Sticks

*for Jameen Kaur*

My thoughts are a bad-tempered waitress
slamming down meals made
by a poorly-paid chef who's working for cash
and doesn't give a toss about the eggs
he breaks or cooks, and my waitress
wears cheap black slacks a cheap black blouse
and cheap black shoes and she makes
cheap slack swipes at tables with a half-wet cloth
to earn a half-wage for her half-work
she knows that's all it's worth
she is half-jaded half-untapped and she swipes
my half-full plate away when I am less than sated
and it's a shame to waste it
and she's the shame, she refills my bitter cup
with some fake drink that'd I'd do well to use
as fuel to burn my half-life mid-life diaries with tonight
she's my mind and minder, she's the same
as the undone things I should have
and the ones I slacked on and left half done
she's used to sleeping on her feet
to going unnoticed across borders
and that's not all she's used for
she's the steam on rainy windows
she's mildew slowly forming
she's the smell of a little too little hygiene
a little too much later, she's my mind
in all its forms and glories
in all its twisted goriness she is IT
the giddy bitch, she's the slaughterer
a part time carcass-dresser on a back-to-work scheme,
the stigmata on hands that have half been places
they shouldn't have and never came back
she's my tired feet, she's the waitress in service
she's bringing me thoughts
and I am waiting on her.

# Canonisation

in his defence
he's been conducting his own show trials
since memory existed and before
and he always represents himself –
he's been juror,
judge and prosecution,
he's been witness
and oh has he been victim,
he has accused us crimes of commission,
of omission and the crime of our existence
in our sin we stand before him,
sure we can't help our foolish selves

he's spilled things he shouldn't under oath
he's let out-of-bag-cats mewl across courtrooms
while he spoke and then said he didn't own them
and that in fact if we knew anything about him
we'd have known he's always been allergic

he's claimed diminished responsibility
and then he's claimed guilt
he's claimed just-cause right after
he perjured himself for us
and as he detailed what it was
we'd done or hadn't
he might occasionally have hit upon the truth
this wasn't his intention though
in this courtroom
truth is what matters least
it's never what really happened that's at issue
it's getting the conviction
and then offering us forgiveness
for our weakness,
for our human failings;
he's a bona-fide latter-day saint.

# Serotonin

*for Stephen Murray*

It began from fear of the moment sleep hits
that unbearable inescapable loss of everything
convinced me to undertake an occupation
of the half-deserted cities of the world at night-time,
I took to night-walking that harsh year in darkness
I occupied the fear of falling, of sleeping
I occupied the equal terrors of waking or not waking
I escaped from lying in my stacked-box apartment, fearing
the horror of sounds seeping from other people's radios
from the sheltered ughs of their futile attempts at lovemaking
I evaded thoughts of all the irons in all the buildings
that might not have been unplugged and the resultant infernos
I didn't smell charred flesh in my nostrils as I drifted or fear the perfection
of carbon monoxide poisoning; I was outside walking.

I didn't have to dwell on thoughts of creeping black cancer
colonising my lungs or strangling my arteries, that year I walked
under sodium lights or in darkness on three continents
I embraced the menace of white-teeth billboards' grimaces
I took to them that harsh year of urban foxes and early morning refuse trucks.
It was my year of homeless people's frozen dozing on cardboard corners
of unaccustomed drunks swaying out from emblazoned night clubs
my year of swallowing the heart scald and the savagery of city streets
at night time, of the beauty of rain on tarmac and headlights
and neon signage seeping, of litter drifting on wind gusts in car parks.

All that year I collapsed in daylight onto laundered hotel linen
where I dreamt of serotonin whilst my credit card kept paying
as the year drew closed I stroked my skin for the velvet, sluggish feel of it
and extracted remnants from my bank account and flew home
but even on the journey I was sleep starved and greedy for it
I was splayed out on airport benches yawning, I put my head
on ketchup-stained tables in fast food courts and dozed there
and when I got home I started sleeping nocturnally and I concede
that it's usual, it's normal to get lazy towards evening but now
I can't look in the face of mornings; sleep is my narcotic
I would inject it in public but instead I must wait here
through midday, through dull afternoons and through teatime
for the moment when sleep hits and swallows me.

# Cat Come Down

*in memory*

This late and this full of it you come round
and you're buzzing at the light shades
flying into windows like something I captured
in a jam jar and then set free in this small apartment,
you are hopping off the walls and this isn't a poem about drugs
it's about your sudden certainties
that the world's now on your wavelength
and all things are possible in love, in lust, in business
when it hasn't moved an inch from where it was this morning
when you couldn't feed the meter for your heating,
so you came here because you had to share this (and it is warmer)
and I say no! no! come down cat, calm down cat
but you're soaring and won't be talked down
you say you'll fly from whatever ledge you're on
and you're brimming with excitement
you are first up for precipice jumping
with a million ideas flying you always lack specifics
and I don't know if I could tell the difference
between ordinary optimism and your self-destructive urges
but I feel of weight and clay and earth, I feel your senior
and who's to blame for it? Has someone inflated you?
If so I wish like hell they hadn't because it's manic
and not good for you but you're high on it and
it's infectious; even though I know everything about this
I am not impervious, so I say one last time
cat come down, cat come down
let's set about calming you
I say the put-the-kettle-on things
I say the let's-sleep-on-it things
the you-can-have-the-sofa-bed-and-stay-here-with-me things
but no you are wired and this night is for walking
you take me parading out into it, you are contagious
and I catch it, then I am laughing – you are helium
and it is everywhere, your hand slips my way
so I kiss your palm while you laugh out loud and we swing

arm in arm out past the junctions, we keep walking
under street lights and on over the Quincentennial bridge
with its black water shining under it
and our breath plumes myth-making out ahead of us
we are fire-breathing dragons
burning all the darkness in the universe
until our bubble bursts that is.

# Harvesting Underwater

The collie doesn't smell good up close
but she's ten paces ahead, trotting, and I'm okay with that.
She makes a valuable contribution to
the salt-wind-silage and damp-earth smells,
she gives off the tang of sweetness
of dead things and history which factual as it might be
is no great predictor of the future nor even any
good indicator of what I could harvest beneath the water
in these submerged fields.

We happened on them with no warning
when we aced the hilltop, both of us running, collie lightfoot
and me overfed and floundering, but there on the cusp of it
bent over gasping, these sprat-silver fields of water
opened like a tundra, like grassland flowing nowhere
and even the dog was startled.
If she was a Springer she'd have plunged in,
but collie dog paused to reassure herself
that what was different didn't matter then went on
about her business, wafting.

I imagine I am walking, arms out on the stone wall-tops
that I can see appearing and re-submerging mid-sea
like rucks in a bedspread or someone's early summer affectations.
A lesson as easily learned as it's forgotten is
that one should never make firm plans for nature,
it just happens and you have to see
if what is different matters
and if not then go on about your business.

If you stand here and inhale it you'll realise that yes,
the air has sweetness, dead things and history in it
but it's November first and this air has winter in it, believe me
it's bringing it, don't let that rancid yellow sky-bound icon fool you,
it will be gone soon. I can smell it
decaying.

# I Imagine an Army

It is very seldom one meets anyone
from the old country now,
and even when we do chance to coincide
on some foreign-controlled street
our eye contact is furtive and hurried.

Still though, every day at four
I put my uniform on and lace up
my patent leather shoes then
I imagine a parade ground
I imagine an army
and I march, turn, salute.

# Loose Lips Sink Ships

this girl couldn't make love unless
someone would talk to her – I didn't judge her
there's no one alive who doesn't
have something that bothers them
and I fancied myself as a suitable candidate –
someone who met her verbosity criteria
though she took some convincing, in truth
it shouldn't have worked for us;
when she'd researched it she decided
no smokers, asthmatics or people afflicted
with any respiratory deficiencies would cut it
but I made a clean fist of it, first I took out
my inhalers and showed them, then I recited
a whole rosary without breathing,
to finish it off I mock bowed and made the sign of the cross
and it seems my performance
or something about me grabbed her
she needed someone who could keep talking
she said, while they made love to her
who could blue streak at her
someone who wouldn't leave any gaps
for her heart to fill in or her pulses,
so I didn't; the first time I babbled
I whispered, I urged and at certain pertinent moments
I orated, Martin Luther King couldn't have equalled it
but when she was sated I paused just for a minute
but she gripped me and said 'no slacking,
don't stop! Quick, quick I need you to speak to me'
– she was scared of her heart she said
scared of the sound of her blood in her ears
and the pulse at her wrist
so I spouted a few Yeats lines between kisses
and I went Adrienne Rich in the crook of her elbow
and I trotted out spells from Macbeth's witches
and a few telly advert jingles
but something in her skin and her lustre caught me

and I lingered transfixed at her temple
and as my lips stilled her eyes filled and she said,
'you have to go now – I thought we'd be different
when I couldn't get a word in
but you haven't lived up to it,'
so I talked a blue streak again
but she silenced me ever so sadly,
later I bought her a radio
but she wasn't having that either.

# Lobotomised

I had a lover once, one of those ones you live in like an island,
most people thought her female and spoke of her with 'she's'
but actually I never spotted that, she was always male for me
she was jawed and tongued and grooved and had tear trail rivers
down his cheeks, she was lived in — every inch the man about town
her mouth jutted like a sea port gawping open, she'd a jaw
of unburnt stubble like so many dead autumn fields and he thought
pretty highly of himself his-torically speaking thought himself
a singing dancing storytelling half-hero half-villain half queen,
but things between the head and heart got themselves conflicted
and in the choice between amputation and lobotomy she took
what he thought was the least worst option and demonstrated
the problems inherent in consensual decision making.

# A Plague On All Our Houses

It's Saturday morning on the flaggy shore
in storm Darwin's aftermath
and the wind has a kick to it like
Padraic Ó Conaire's donkey or
John Charles McQuaid's compassion for me
and I can't see where the road used to be
for all these refugee boulders
it's strewn like a warzone, with rubble
like Kiev this morning reduced
to a contest between dollars
and euros and roubles and people,
and I don't know which side I'm on
in these hexagonal conflicts,
here at the shoreline it's cold-grey and billowy
but without blinking the news headlines
could tell me it's tropical, it all depends
which way the wind's blowing (thanks Bob)
and what particular god they are serving
and I'm no passerby, here in the Burren
to genuflect at rockscapes or to build
tiny Buddhist temples in the path of the sun.
Me? I believe you can make a god
out of anything people will kneel for
and I'm used to these regions their harshness
the cattle, the bishops and widows
the May the first *piseogs*, I am familiar
with these tuberculosis villages and let's say
that nothing has caught me off guard
except how bitter these days are
and for all our talk of borders
how fragile our maps are: now even this karst
is impermanent and no disrespect
but I want to remember these times
without metaphor, without interference or censorship
but it's midday and the Angelus peals from my radio
it tells me you get what you pay for
it tells me you get what you pay for
or what you can see your way to take.

41

# Flags of Convenience

by chance I met Linden and his pal Matt
who he introduced as
a Belfast-Presbyterian-Delhi-man
and a half-hearted vegetarian at that.
We met in an Indian restaurant
where tables were squeezed in tight
so we shook hands and set to chatting
over naan bread and lentils
we talked economics, new Irish television series
and the strange cultures of the Irish in America
we got somehow to the topic of Quaker-owned factories
and debated if one of these
was or wasn't Rowntree MacIntosh
then we hit on the flags and Lambegs
on the imminent arrival of Richard Haass
coming in from Brooklyn to tell the locals
what to do about their symbols
we remarked on traditions under threat
and Linden said that for youngsters
the policy of parity means they can't follow
their fathers into heavy industry;
we skirmished a bit about that one
about whether it was economic and general
caused by the downturn in manufacturing
but Linden said no, no, the fault was
positive discrimination
and a way of living ending
and he elevated himself
ever so slightly from his chair to defend inheritance
but then he relented and said more gently
there's not a wild amount of women has an interest in business
you're a rare one he said and I said Linden man
you are a dinosaur, you're an extinct species
but I said it without rancour
we sailed that evening under flags of convenience
and didn't drop anchor.

# There Has Been No Breach of Conduct or Discipline Found

not when they called you 'Mary' and 'faggot' in Rossport,
irrespective of the fact that it was an inspector who did it
there were no breaches, sure, these things can get heated
and it's not like they're trained for it is it? Or paid like?
And on the spur of the moment when they threatened
to break your car windows, they were discipline personified.
When they whacked the back of your neck with a baton
they conducted themselves with decorum and just got mixed up
between what legs were and heads were, anatomy isn't easy
sure you'd have to accept that and they aren't doctors –
they're grand lads and lassies and never more so than when
they use their great sense of humour and joke about deporting
or raping a few girls they met up at camp, they're grand lads
having a bit of disciplined banter wouldn't anyone? And didn't
they get hold of Margaretta and make our streets safer
by conducting her jailwards, no don't be too down on them
there have been no breaches of anything ever.

# Obitchuary

*for Tracy Geraghty*

This time I will speak ill of the dead
but not of the skeletons she made of Northern streets
not the skeletons of men who starved in Ireland
nor the thin men with viruses she stigmatised –
ostracised first, and then criminalised.
I will speak out about the Argentinean dead
all shot in their backs, and about Pinochet
who she supported and his helicopters spewing corpses
into the sea and the torture, the hubris
of only negotiating with certain classes of 'terrorist,'
I will speak ill of the markets she loosed
to feed on the carcasses of families and homes
in bleak towns she'd wrecked, and of the puppets
she sent out with batons or war planes,
I will curse her and them and our own slick proxies
who learned all they know in her classroom
and are right now in action, let it be said
that I am happy she's gone
I am glad Thatcher's dead,
but let's not leave it at that,
let's make this a watershed.
Let this be our watershed.

# Shopkeeper

*for Sunny Jacobs (the real Dalai Lama)*

My grand aunt was the queen of gobstoppers
and St Anthony and even if she stretched things
to their limits she'd never tell a lie –
she told me 'arrah what the hell does right mean
when good oozes from wrong decisions'
in her fags and sweets and bread and milk den
she was the queen of shop-cakes and ice-breakers,
when I ran in to tell her of a brother's rampaging
or an older sister empire-building with my playthings
she said '*a stor* justice well it's not just us who knows it
and you'd do well to listen instead of always talking.'

When she was found face down surrounded
by milk bottles and IOUs she shouldn't have accepted,
the *plámásers* came in droves, fresh-washed
and unfamiliar with such sadness, she left us
with battles raging over who it was that loved her
but they were fruitless, she was no partisan
no side-taker, she died alone in a sea of muck-rakers
saying it's no use being sectarian.

# Gorse

Your tight lips and stubborn back
and the sound of our dinner dishes
being none too gently stacked
have sent me outside
to sneak a cigarette
in the closest thing a summer night has
to darkness.

My match strike flares
and blinds me for an instant
as I guiltily inhale.
Down on the bogland
below our house
there are car lights moving slowly,
then going out.
A door thuds shut
and no other sound comes up.

Close by my ear I hear
your bare feet lub-dub-ing like my heartbeat
across the wooden kitchen floor.
My nicotine plumes fray
then disappear,
and on the uplift of the breeze
an acrid petrol smell
mingles with the wildflower, gorse
and wet earth fumes.

In the morning all there is
is wood smoke and a few blackened patches,
otherwise the gorse bushes
stand out flag-yellow
and unmolested.

Bogland doesn't always burn
that easily, even after
a surprise late-night baptism with petrol
up here, where we are, a sly sea mist
sometimes sneaks in to douse it
and it's left to smoulder
neither burning nor put out
like we are
like we are.

# Seer

I see things in advance of them happening and I'm tired of it

Subtext:
What I never say is true

Context:
Whatever ever happened still exists

Promise:
I'll offer you honesty

Excuse:
I won't come through (*insert selected reason here* _____)

Fact:
I would have to get too near you to forgive

Lie:
I didn't mean it to end this way

Epilogue:
I saw it coming

Postscript:
I see things, me.
I told you.

# Scrapes

She likes the wrenches
the gasps and the shatters
the wrong things
the pain waves
the skin breaks
the skull-burning hair pulls
she likes them.

She likes sidesteps
ducking round corners
rough edges
and wastelands
she likes wall-leaning
the scrape of some chancer's stubble
the sirens? She knows them
the sound
of a head hitting concrete,
no matter who did it —
she likes it.

She likes the nerves
when she walks home
at night time
ballpoint at the ready
and she'd do it;
straight for the eyeball
you better believe it
she's five foot nothing
and trouble, she's trouble
and she'll make sure
you know it.

# Pollero

I was crossing my own borders with no visa when we met
I cut the wire fence between my chest and neck
ran low across the desert with all of my senses on alert,
I camped out in the stomach region until the searchers
quenched their lights, slammed car doors and left,
in the dust plumes their wheels threw up
I fled lower still and snaked my way through scrubland
until I landed in the shadows of my groin,
there were others there before me I should've known,
they took it upon themselves to show me how things were done
and illegals must adapt fast so I caught on,
it was as good a spot as any to be based
there was no going back, no other place
this was a flat land and it was safe; anyone approaching
could be seen from miles away
their tired footfall noises would pulse warnings through
my blue-veined wrists and towards my heart
in the distance, these incomers always looked like children,
but when they neared they'd age until they stood
beside me husk-rattling and shrunk, and they would not bring gifts
or bribes or graft just plastic bags and backpacks full of phone numbers
for someone somewhere who might help
and they would beg for water in frenzies of thirst
that sometimes saw them glug from polluted sources,
from dysentery fountains that would drown them later
while they squatted in barren desert regions in situations
not of their own making,
one group of no-different pilgrims came here
and you came gasping in their midst but you didn't speak or touch
so I surmised that you'd died already in one of the many ways
we have for passing from this life to the next,
you consumed your water though, you dog-lapped it
and ate some beans and rice then you loitered quietly for me
I had no license to inquire what your silence held at bay
until the day you ran dead fingers through my hair and clutched me
by my forearm with your fingers sunk in deep

and it says something about endurance about innocence
that when you pushed me down
I had it in me to be disappointed –
I was momentarily disappointed,
but that's the custom here and I am long since accustomed
to such treatment, in fact sometimes in its absence
I have found I miss it, so I let you knock me
I hid my eyes I hid my bitter throat and you spoke as if in warning,
as one well-used to talking you said 'if a desert flower's wilting
quench its thirst but if fire's burning get yourself out first'
and I would have asked you something then,
but you, too, took what you wanted and went on.

# Shrinking

Yesterday I was the same size as my wheelie bin
but today I cannot even reach its lid,
I had to lob the last of last night's dinner skywards
and trust blind fate that it would go in,
last week I had to put cushions on my car seat
and can now just about see out – if I sit up straight that is
and at breakfast from my new perspective I spotted
that you have a prematurely sagging chin
but I thought it better not to mention it, on dressing
I found that closer than usual examination of my toes
was possible and that my trousers had to be rolled up,
meaning, seemingly, that my height-to-weight distribution ratio
is not particularly stable, not one to let things
progress without at least attempting intervention
I got my overalls, a spanner and as a precaution
I stuck a lump-hammer in my belt and in I went
to sort it out, not unexpectedly I found that entering
my own mouth cavity was a squeeze but I persisted
and was rewarded by access to the more generously
proportioned oesophagus where it was dark and rank
and I wished I'd brought a head torch or some form
of illumination but when my eyes eventually adjusted
I went to flick the switch for growth and shrinkage
and sure enough I found it jammed but much more firmly
than I'd anticipated, I greased it, to no avail, I wrenched it
and yes I know this seems indelicate but I got the hammer out
and belted it – the famous last resort of DIY experts;
IF ALL ELSE FAILS JUST BASH IT, and with a shudder
it gave way – a flap behind it opened and I discovered
that I was in some storage area where it seems
I keep my unsaid responses to all our interactions
and listen this isn't flattering but I found a bunch
of pre-packed utterances that wanted to berate you
so I diagnosed myself with diminution: I know now
that the time we spend together is the source
of my stature difficulties, what I am trying to say is
that I'm leaving and it's your fault, I mean
I'm shrinking here, who on earth could blame me?
If this goes on I'll vanish.

# Dad Learns a New Word: Circa 1981

It showed up with some other new words
like rough patch, emancipation and
'you mind them so – you wanted six children'
mostly, these meant Dad making lunch
and us sometimes going to his office
where Nuala the secretary was delegated
to mind us, not feminism I know, for the purists,
but that was the deal as we knew it and for us
this feminism thing meant more law and order
than we'd been used to; he'd been a boarder
in Clongowes, seen and not heard, but we'd
been told *mol an óige agus tiocfaidh siad* and
resultantly didn't take too kindly to structure.

Patriarch as he was known then in our house,
spent his time confounded that six children
were people with different opinions and
every single one got a voicing; his job no more than
to listen, referee the worst scrapes and feed us.
No matter if he wanted perfection or discipline –
starting a row about 'no reading books at the table' or
'I won't have that dog in the kitchen while we're eating'
meant, not that it would all be adjusted to suit him
but he'd get a rebellion and should have let
sleeping dogs lie or just stay in the kitchen while
we were eating, poor Dad became a feminist,
eventually, by conceding that with children
keeping them alive is as good as perfection.

# Gawk

*for Mick McCaughan*

There was this one time
in a place called Pie de la Cuesta
near Acapulco, I had this bird, right
classy she was, muy elegante
and a beak on her like
you wouldn't believe
and legs, hombre woohee!
legs de chinga tu madre,
those days I was drinkin and up for it
muy muy listo, you know?
But things got pretty wild in 'pulco
so sticking to the coastline
an turning my back to no one
I headed out of town
and that's when I met her
ah Pie de la Cuesta,
she was down on the beach
watching the red sun
that very first evenin
she was wadin in the shallows
and then later just standin there
with one a them legs raised
and hombre I am no poet but te digo
with the sunset blood red and poolin
out on the horizon, and them golden lights
winkin 'cross the water at us
and the waves that kept on comin
and the whole world sinkin lower
well I fell straight for her
I couldn't but watch her
and when those pony boys
had rounded up their hosses
cantered away up streetside
all hollerin' and happy and when
the hawkers had given up on

selling their trinkets and they left me
on the warm sand there
I went to her and man oh man,
she didn't resist me,
the earth shifted
the worm turned
and I won't forget her
my gawky thin-legged sea bird;
when I get out of here
I'm gonna get a tattoo of her
right here, see?
On my shoulder.

# There's Only One Interchangeable Poem

While I was thinking of the world's one and only interchangeable poem
I asked if you remembered the day all those horses got electrocuted
at the races? Remember? For a while no one knew what had happened,
they just circled and collapsed one by one on the fake-grass parade ring.
What I think is, isn't it a wonder no one tried to resuscitate them
– was that just lack of imagination?

While you were thinking about the horses my phone rang
and I answered. But it was my brother not someone important
and now he's trying to convince me that there's a market
for small nodding models of politicians that people
could stick on their dashboards and he says
it's not commerce he's talking that it's revolution
because when people are driving and listening to drivel spewing
from their radios the nodding and bobbing of his small caricatures
will stop anyone from paying attention to shock jocks
and so the politicians could wax lyrical about deficits
and all the people in traffic would smirk at them
instead of sacrificing their children,
and the worst thing is I can see them selling and him doing it
and there's something I should feel about it
I see things, me, but I don't often feel them.

In a different story, a man at the supermarket looked at me and spoke,
he was an old bloke and he told me that a small circular path
leads everyone back to the start then he looked down at his shoes
so I looked down too but there was nothing of note there
just brown shoes that we stared at together for a moment or two
on the tarmac outside a supermarket which was the half-stocked
bastard child of a hypermarket, he said he was waiting
and that it took up most of his time these days, 'Wait' he said
and I did but he said no more and shortly was led by his arm to a car
by a woman you'd never connect with him
I wanted him to say something in conclusion
but he just got in the car and they swept off
since this is fiction though, I can insert it,

except that some days it's hard to know which lies to tell about what,
but I could call him the poet who knew
that there has only ever been one interchangeable poem,
and who told me so in the car park of a supermarket
but you know as soon as I've written it, I've lost interest

except for a the bit that comes later, where a girl in search
of a new interpretation of this one poem of all poems,
cuts words out from a piece of brown felt and wears them in a pouch
on a string on her neck, and she'll tell me the options are limitless,
with just those words and their letters and my various humours
but of her there's not much to say except
that she wore a pouch on a string on her neck
and I liked the way her fingers curled on her teacup when
she leaned over towards me, I replay that sometimes in my head
when I'm walking, mostly, and the fact that I never bothered
arranging the words for us to get to that point in the story, to there
in the café where she leaned over towards me makes no odds to us;
I mean you have to fill your head with something and who ever said
there has to be character development? In the non-fiction
workaday world I find that there frequently isn't and now I suppose
you want me to make you feel something?
Make you engage with this? Well one day in the café
when there were no spare seats and a headache was banging my temples
I sat beside a girl who was meek-looking, not overly pretty,
but then neither am I and she started talking and I started to listen,
'I have all the words in the world at my disposal' she said,
'what I'm missing is order or sequence' and I gathered
that she was not meek, that in fact she was mischievous and so
I incorporated that information whilst she waited to see
what response I'd concoct for her, I took a sip of my tea
to buy time with and she said 'Do you ever make lists of things?'
And when I said I did she said 'See we were fated to meet
on this day in this place at this table' and feeling it was time
I made some contribution I said 'There's no arguing with fate is there?'
and she said 'There's nothing I like less than a good loser
would you ever fuck off and don't humour me.'

Then she leaned towards me all open hearted and said
'I've every word in the world on a string round my neck
and we're going out together to use them' and there were words
on the street, words on the bus seats, words in the crevices
of the flat concrete pavement and when we woke up
there words on the bed sheets.
For days after that I was picking stray syllables
from the floor of my room and making poems with them
she was such a substantial occurrence that I couldn't but write about her
so I had poems, but the girl who had all the words in the world
well there was no sign of her. Now do you care about her?
And if I said I was both parts of the dialogue, would that matter?

While I was thinking again of the world's one poem
I met a girl on the street who was a one-act play that I starred in;
rabid, I thought, that's what she is, this must be a tragedy
she had a white chalky substance dried in the corners of her lips
walk away, walk away I told myself, legs already braced for departure
but she said; 'You know fuck all about this' and I listened.
Someone on the street near us was using a jackhammer
in a nerve-shattering staccato, to me it seems pointless
breaking up a pavement like that. She said it again;
'You know fuck all about this' and I tried 'You're probably right' but
I had her bitten-nailed hand on my sleeve then and she'd stepped nearer
she leaned her face towards mine with her chin jutting out
like a ship prow, this won't, I thought, go anywhere good
so I felt in my pocket hoping to draw out some coins or something
to give to this child-witch who had me cornered in broad daylight in public
Fuck, I said. Fingers, my own if that matters, scrabbled the depths
of my pocket but they only touched on the warm paper edges of banknotes.
Hoping for the lowest denomination I extracted a note from the bundle.
It was a twenty. Fuck, I said, in such situations language is limited,
she spotted it and as I'd hoped she would she let go of my arm
to get hold of it while I backed away slightly and then stopped.
Keep going I told myself but I was mesmerised, I was stuck there
and she caught the note in both hands and ripped it
right down the middle, then she tore it several more times
until it was in pieces the size of stamps which she scrunched
between her palms until it was unrecognizable as any sort
of a currency 'What the fuck do you know about me?' She asked me,

now speaking more quietly, and she let the note in its segments
fall to the ground, to the footpath between us, where it fluttered
and then dispersed itself while we watched it; she was no stranger
to mining the drama from an occasion, this girl.
I stood there. Well I did. I was wrong-footed and knew it
so I sighed at the injustice of being confronted
about an internal preconception in daylight,
I stood like a martyr and she looked at me
then spat on the ground, wet patches were spreading at her armpits
her upper lip's downy fair hair was beginning to glisten with moisture
I couldn't take my eyes off her. She walked off, she swung up the street
past the general post office leaving my body contorted in tension.
I drew breath and straightened my jacket sleeve
as if this would reclaim my physique for myself from a predator
I felt overrated; I looked around though and there was nothing
but a mess of the usual taxis with engines ticking over
a few bored cops looking gormless and a couple of hipsters
practicing gauche postures on the pedestrian, paved centre,
no one took any notice of me and why would they? Did I say that?
That no one was watching except my own internal spectator,
I checked my pockets, I could make sense of a robbery
and just then it was sense I was after, my phone was where it should be
my wallet untouched, and I could make no sense at all of it.
I thought of calling someone. Who? I don't know and what would I say?
I've no idea. I took a deep breath, and walked on 'Hey you'
she'd called from her spot by the wall and it's funny but I knew
straight away it was me she was talking to, there's something
of that about me and sure enough she pulled herself upright
and came my way without looking at any of the dozens and dozens
of people around us all consumed in their busyness.
'You' she'd said 'You know fuck all about this.' And what if I said
I was both parts of the dialogue? What of it?
Still and all though I'm glad you didn't see me.

And the Professor calls this postmodernism, says it's institutional
it helps him not see things, how handy is that for him?
But it means that he thinks he is right
and if he is then he must think it's something
but that's one step too far for his musings and he knows
that he could seduce students. He doesn't. But the fact that it might come

with his territory and that he could do it inflates what he thinks
of himself and when he and the others are peer-reviewing,
the fact that they feel they've the power of seduction seems
to be built into what they think about what they say about anything,
if I could insert the old bloke; the poet of all poets from the car park
of the shrunk-raisin hypermarket and I could be bothered to flesh him out
so you would believe that those guys would listen to him,
he'd say there's only ever been one interchangeable poem
and they'd know what he meant and how it related to potency
but he didn't say that, I did and I don't know if
I even believe it/ I'm utterly certain of it/make what you will of that.

# Cross My Heart

~~we say no you hang up and many~~
~~other stupid cutesy things~~
~~we leave parties early to go home~~
~~sometimes it's better for everyone if we're alone~~
~~we are cloying and we don't ever fight~~
~~we are sweet hands clasped tight~~
~~we finish each other's sentences we're in rhyme~~
~~and we ruin each other's punch lines all the time~~
~~in the cinema we don't care what film we see~~
~~we sicken people by sitting there knee to knee~~
~~on Sundays we leave the dishes in the sink~~
~~and get up late, worse we've been together~~
~~much much longer than you think~~
~~we know each other's weak spots~~
~~we know each other's sub plots~~
~~we ignore each other's dark side~~
~~and we avoid the places hurt hides~~
but it came to find us then
count to ten you told me:
before you answer
count to ten.

# Solutions to Homelessness

*for Rita Ann Higgins*

Sure can't you live in the drainpipes?
Or on one of those windowsills with the thin metal spikes on them
if the pigeons can manage it, I don't see your problem
are you a bird or a man? Can't you fold yourself
into the ashtray of an old Nissan Micra,
these days no one is smoking
so I'd say they're all vacant, can't you sleep in a chip punnet
or better a snack box with a lid?
Sleep in Eyre Square sure where Pádraic Ó Conaire used to be,
or if you stood in Browne's doorway that might keep
the rain off you, think outside of the box for once can't you?
You could sleep in a lobster pot or on the back
of a swan down in Claddagh,
you could line up a few ducks and lie down on them
maybe you could sleep on the mudguard
of one of those crooked-wheel bicycles the two Belgians left
to be vandalised, or you could tell the Guards at Mill Street
that you're there to report a white-collar criminal
it would be decades before someone could see you,
and at least you'd have a roof over you while you waited
maybe you could study something in the Open University
while you're there in the waiting room, and better yourself
you could build yourself into one of Macnas's puppets
you'd surely get at least the summer out of it,
and if you're not fond of the arts can't you sleep in the fountain
– you'd be showered and all then, you could furl yourself
in the sail of a yacht down at the docks
or if you got a small trolley with wheels and you lay on it,
you could sleep in one of the segments
of the revolving doors in the Meyrick Hotel without blocking anyone
will you go away and don't bother me
there is no housing crisis in Galway for anyone
with even a shred of imagination, will you show some initiative,
even snails can find homes for themselves.

# I Spy With Your Little Eye…

If I flew across the dim space between
the Reek and my own upturned face
or if I flew belly-low in the winter sky
brushing down over the dusk-pink sea
between Mweelrea and myself, would
my bird's eye show me why I stood
stock still where all the currents meet
watching a heron shake cramps from
his redundant leg then hop and swap them
so he she or it stands there rearranged but
more or less the same or would I grow engines
and leave vapour traces to evaporate
as my undercarriage groaned itself erect
for our descent towards Knock,
and would I see me there? Or here,
standing with the heron in the current
in this evening light, would I see that
from the window seat where I sit now
nose pressed against the pane?

# Packing Shellfish

I can picture one-eyed Sean,
with a scar made stark by
the skin-stretching cold reaching
down the side of his watery nose,
then trailing away in the patchy
white stubble waste of his cheek,
he smelled more like
the sea than the sea does.

I can picture him across from me
in the damp dripping bunker,
a butcher's slab table between us
laid out with stacks of creaking Styrofoam boxes
all full with trapped furious lobsters
black and blue-ish.

I can see the uppermost ones
wave their useless defences,
claws clamped now – neutered
with heavy duty rubber bands,
I can imagine me – looking down,
like you must, when packing
either lobsters or crays, to prevent
your cold fingers becoming victims
of shellfish anger.

I can see my red chapped hands,
and the wet cuffs of a sweatshirt,
rubbing my wrists in the glare of
a strip light and a dark square
of night-time outside the double doors,
and I can hear murmurs travelling
in, from the men doing the loading.

To me and Sean grading at the table,
the sounds seem to be seeping from
red cigarette tips floating
like punctuation through
the straining noises men make
when they're lifting.

The same men, cleaner and
less surefooted in treacherous shoes,
carried his coffin on a blistering day
in November. Sean the bachelor was packed
like a lobster, he was loaded then sent
and after twenty-two years
of him doing the grading, Tommy
took it over that evening.

# How To Not See

*for Vicky Donnelly who's fixing everything.*


In Spanish controlled Cueta I heard
that if you roll yourself up
like an orange and try to dimple your skin
if you really get into it, think of pips
and segments and citrus, you can get
into a fridge truck and then onto a ferry
for Europe proper where
you may or may not perish.


In Berlin just off Hannah Arendt Street
curious children made mazes
of concrete memorials
and I found myself hoping
they'd never get back
to wherever we are.


From the island of Lindau
I swam in Lake Constance
and didn't think for a minute
about the accumulation of wealth
– the price tags on the items
I fingered under the eyes of the shop mistress
undoubtedly helped with this,
and as for lake swimming which is
cost-neutral and borderless
well I can't quite recommend it,
it's like bathing in syrup
then rolling in flour and frying yourself.


Back in Munich after my tour of Dachau
I found that I'd run out of metaphor
and for a time everything was itself
no more or no less, then in order
to stop me from running in terror
from the city's inhabitants I went to the park

where young men surfing the Eisbach
were riding the same wave over and over again
and I stayed there until I remembered
how to not see things.

Yes I tell you come live in Dublin
where our ministers look at us
in ways that communicate
the same contempt that would see us
dismembered with our separate, dirty limbs
severed and spewing out of helicopters
if we lived somewhere or somewhen
less visible.

In Cueta I heard that if you roll up
like an orange and try to dimple your skin
if you really get into it – think of pips
and segments and citrus, you can get
on a fridge truck for Europe where
our ministers dream of themselves
mounted on equestrian statues
in plazas de soberanía
and where we won't torture you
except when we force you
to peel your own skin
and feed on yourself.

# Gullible

I met the take-it-back man down at the shopping centre
he was soap-boxing, waxing lyrical and I drank his potion.
It was said that it could cure the worst of all the words
you'd ever spewed out in fury or in disappointment
or if a cure was beyond the bounds of such elixirs
it could reclaim the offending utterances and put them
in storage as long as you swallowed and didn't spit that is
it could make happenstances fall from their standing,
go over old ground and make it new. It could undo
the damage your sharp tongue had inflicted
on the unsuspecting, the suspicious and the blameless,
it could pale the blushes from each stupid outburst before
they ever hit your cheekbones, if that is you took
two small mouthfuls and vowed to stay quiet for
the duration of their troubled ingestion, it would banish shame
before it ever hit your tonsils and traipsed its way
down your resistant gullet, I know it sounds far-fetched
but I for one swallowed it.

# Doubtless

Up Dame Street I went being very careful
to believe everything I saw there, on past
the castle went I, then I winked at Christ Church
and swiftly bended one knee in St Pat's Cathedral
a young buck outside Burdock's had his own hands
down inside his tracksuit waistband and though
he needed only seven euros for a bed, he was
more surprised than anything to receive it –
not me sure: I believed him. Over I went across
and on the river I walked, not having any need
for bridges and begging your credence
there was nothing beneath me but clear water
and shopping trolleys until the air at the Four Courts
let me down gently and there I remembered
quite recent days of doubting and whilst
I wouldn't quite call them cravings there was
at least the tang, that grasp on my saliva from
my half-beaten addiction to doubting, it seems
I didn't kill it even if I did give it one hell of a kicking.
I skidded on the gravel at O'Connell Bridge,
saluted big Jim and Daniel in passing, you'd think
at least they'd answer but when I passed the news stands
and saw the headlines on the papers hollering on
about the world athletics championships I got to thinking
about cheerleading and no I wasn't disbelieving
but the notion that someone or other could spend
a decade back-flipping, perfecting it, it just to add
one more tumble to their earlier world record seemed
a bit pointless but I'm dissembling which is not a symptom
of someone saying something they have faith in
and rather than be thought of as an unconvinced
or agonising agnostic I stopped at Store Street station
and proclaimed to the hopeful assembled that,
categorically, I had no doubts at all about anything
though I don't know if they believed me.

# Her Sisters Remember It Differently

But then again they would wouldn't they? The ones
who are older say their little sister bore the brunt of it though
she doesn't see it like that. She prefers thinking of them dancing
in the kitchen with both parents singing and her up late
on a school night when she should have been sleeping,
but they said they were in training for Broadway, for stardom
and not to tell anyone. She prefers stowaway games where
they hid in the attic as quiet as mouses, as mices, as meeses,
or the adventures she invented at Granny's while her mother
was away singing opera, in Paris or London or Rome
and she prefers how important she felt in the schoolyard
when the others were taunting but she was the only one
who knew the reason her Da had got scarcer was because
of his extremely important work as a spy and if she said
where he was to anyone they all might die
and she'd crossed her heart anyways so she wasn't saying,
she likes to remember reciting poems she'd learned off in school
to pirates on shore leave down at the bar in the docks,
how her Da had brought her and none of her sisters
and how that night he'd held her so tightly and not let her get further
in case those seafaring varmints would steal her
and make her queen of the seas but he wouldn't let them,
no chance of it, not in his lifetime; he'd slay 'em like dragons,
like vagabonds and he'd brought her up Main Street where
they'd sat in the church and lit candles till she started to shiver
and he'd sworn she was destined for fortune, for magnificence
even if he did say so himself and she loved remembering that bit,
she repeated it over and over like when they brought her to visit
her mother she'd say 'Ma we're going to be magnificent, aren't we?'
and they'd all laugh while her mother would hug her.
But her sisters remember it differently.

# Chances Are

trees and cockroaches
will outlive us, tides ignore us
apocalypse will flick us
off as easily as if we were flies
irritating a thin-skinned horse,
this poor beleaguered universe
will continue unencumbered
and the better for it, chances are
that you and I will never be as happy
as we are here doing the crossword
on a train hurtling towards Antwerp,
going for no reason other than to
be together somewhere else.

# Fatigues

I don't wear fatigues for camouflage
or for fashion, I couldn't give a toss
about that macho warlike bullshit
or about your night vision goggles
I don't wear this stuff for boasting
I wear it for survival;
do I have to spell it out?

In order to move forward
I have had to stash
certain things in certain places –
some for safe keeping
and some others that just refuse to leave me
I store my hardcover notebooks
in the button-down thigh pockets
of my combat trousers, in these
I once wrote down the personal experiences
I would most like to dispose of
but each time I tried to park them
it would seem as if they'd vanished
but then they'd write themselves back in
to later episodes and wreak havoc so now
I have to bring them with me and at least
in these clothes I can feel them try to slither
into things from their legside hideouts
long before they do their damage.

In my safari-jungle-issue waistcoat's
many inside pockets I keep all our old photos
yes the same ones I cut you out of
now we lurk there together,
my image and your absence,
which reminds me of how useless
scissors are for cutting some things.

In desert-issue suede boots that don't fit great
I keep blisters more or less the same as anyone's
but I use them differently
they distract me from my hunger
or conversely from the ache I get when sated,
the sharp sting of a flesh wound
is way better than unresolvable heart or stomach ache
as any devotees of self-flagellation
could tell you
but wouldn't.

In case the blisters heal up or scab over
I have inserted some souvenirs of who I was
when I was employable and before you left me
there's a decomposing business card
that reads Area Manager and has my name on it
there's a credit card cut into pieces
so it doesn't function for anything
except exacerbating blisters
and in the instep of the left boot I've put
the keys of the apartment we bought together
they're safe there where no one will touch them
and anyway I hear you've had the locksmith in
so it shouldn't worry you.

My green-ish military style cap is empty
and I hang it from my belt
like a scalp I took from someone
or maybe from myself, I don't wear it but
just in case the way gets dusty or I want
some shadow on my face I keep it close
while I go bare-headed into the future
naked except for the things that I must carry
and I don't mind telling you
their weight sometimes tires me.

# Beetroot Soup

This was one of those awkward off-kilter days
and I was one of the squinters who frowned sideways
at it, not prepared to look at anything directly.
You were one of the wardens, the guardians
checking that things were progressing as
they should be and I sat in my habitual seat
in my usual café and kept my cranky head down
in the paper while you leaned on the counter
and watched me. I felt it on my neck hairs where
it landed and so I murmured fake approval for
the photos of some small-faced politician and
I perused the ads for gadgets that could be used
to improve my golf swing or those beige all in one
leisure suits that I can't imagine anyone wearing,
and I spooned my soup up feigning unfelt relish
for you, my audience, when in fact I consumed it
like a duty instead of appreciating its exoticism and it
was beetroot, thyme and ginger but on a day like this,
a day for not feeling, for not even being it would take
habanero peppers to break through my defences
to surmount my down-day survival mechanisms,
so it was odd then that I found my throat burning
and eyes watering when you said 'listen sorry
for interrupting, pet, but is anything the matter?'

# Background Music

if I could be the faint hum in your ear
of a half-forgotten note
from the half-remembered song
that reminds you of your most gentle self
I would

if I could be the way sheets
lie on your hip bones
during a summer full of light-leaking curtains
or your early-morning eyelids opening to a day
with promise written all over it
I would

if I could come to you in lower-case letters
and be just the right word
and just the right silence
if I could be the correct audible inhalation
at just the right moment
I would

if I could come your way in minor keys
and act a bit more muted
if I could be there hardly noticed
like the feel of your own familiar calf muscle
on your shin bone
while you lie half-sleeping

I would

# Trainspotter

No casual voyeur our man watches lovers
like a birdwatcher would, with binoculars
and territorial maps he notes the peculiarities
of each species, he sometimes camps out
in houses full of history and family pictures
that show off lost days where couples bickered
then smiled for the photos, certain
their sharp words weren't fatal
and in fact were just slight wavers in
an otherwise stable investment, for all
his science though, our love expert doesn't get this
so when he hears raised voices, doors slamming
or when he eavesdrops on our outbursts
of venom and our exaggerated stage-sighs
of exasperation, he writes in his jotter
that this is a relationship in danger when
in fact we were only venting and he received
no invitation to witness, to note-take
in his journal about the hours, the dark nights
and the mornings when us two adversaries
sleep together defenceless, tangled in armistice.

# Bull

Roberto Bolaño rode in
and halted his placid toro mecanico
he threw his leg over the bull's neck
and patted him, while he himself
sat there sidesaddle, then he spoke to us
quoting me first then Nicanor Parra,
then Roque Dalton, then Pablo Neruda,
then Che Guevara, then some Subcomandante
or other and this before I'd even
opened my mouth
or ever put pen to paper,
it's hard isn't it, to get started?

These days he's a corpse though or
a sort of iconic iconoclast
who makes up people to grieve for him –
he's funny like that Bolaño is,
and if I never write anything
it's because he stole my best lines
and binned them
before I'd invented them.

# For Lazarus, Whose Alarm Clock is Ringing

*for Elaine Feeney*

In the airport terminal's time warp the sun-on-glass glare
and the lack of appropriate places to sleep
have left me bug-eyed and pacing static-filled corridors
that send sparks through my fingers and hair
when I touch things (or if I touched things) and I'm thinking
of how we came to be each other's others and how it is
that people like us come to mean things to each other.
Without knowing it does so, the heat from the sun's kiss on
the plate-glass windows licks at my neck, like it we are helpless
our warmth spreads without any permission, we've no borders
no boundaries and we've been friends since we met
so I can say Lazarus get up and talk to me, because I want
to tell you how I'd resolved to be only one person
all of the time until a woman came to my ninth-floor hotel room
and stood at the window looking down at some city below her,
I (or the me I was using) stayed at a distance with my back
to the wall and across those great acres of room space of bed space
and sheet span I watched the light burnish her edges
her ribcage, her jaw and the fine hairs on her arm
and as the evening grew gentler I watched the rise and fall
of her breath while the day itself melted and Lazarus
I wanted to go to her but this me that I've chosen to be
all of the time now didn't know where or how to begin:

I didn't believe that my static-filled fingers
could touch her and she might welcome it and I wanted to tell you
that I mightn't be able to stay being me in situations like this
where I have all the ingredients gathered and measured
and then I forget how to cook them (if that was in fact
me there in the bedroom and not one of my minions)
and I'm saying this because I've learned that staying one person
isn't straightforward and sometimes being truthful is less accurate
than having the courage to act a part beautifully
and Lazarus I want to tell you whenever you get up
that I might not be able and I know you'll know what I mean
because we are each others others and we know things –
Lazarus, it's high time you were up.

# Credentials

Real physical fear? That, I save for love. On Bucareli in Café la Habana, Dec told us that if he could write, really write, 'you know' he said, 'if I could write in a way that would change whoever read my words so that they would never again be who they were before they'd read them; so they couldn't go back,' he said if he could write that way, then he'd write on thin cigarette papers, or in Christmas-cracker fortune-cookie disposable slogan-type locations and when Tim asked 'What about graffiti? Would that do you?' Dec replied that it would be too concrete, too determined. I told them 'I'm afraid I'm not who I said I am.' They both stopped talking and looked at me.

# Homecoming Queen

...in your humpy pine-lined hometown,
I am damaged goods
in the place where you did your underage drinking
your voracious first-and-second cousin kissing
it seems I am the inbred one, the new village idiot
and I'm not who you bargained on me being
when you planned this visit home...

...you act like I have dyke emblazoned
on my forehead, even in the graveyard
you fear your grandparents will
resuscitate themselves and read it,
this makes you cruel; more concerned now
with pleasing people who are long past feeling
than with me standing here offended
but still alive and breathing...

... later in your local
we meet your childhood friends
but I've grown clumsy then and lumpen
and you're humbled from having had
to come here with a gimp like me,
the friends are kind though
they smile and try to chat
with your 'guest from Ireland'
but you see me through a critic's eyes
and to limit any further damage
or the possibility of me saying something gay
you answer every question for me...

...between rounds of darts and heartburn mojitos,
I use my few mis-accented words
on the barman but you only speak
to me in English and when I try
to ease the tension in my neck and shoulders
and head outside to join the smokers

you mutter 'if you smoke that don't think
I'm going to kiss you'
and I don't need anything translated,
I don't need anything translated…

…before I came here with you
being native played in my favour
though it's only now I know this,
in coming here you've got my measure
and it's smaller than we thought; less weighty
in this faltering unsteady latitude
I stand to take my awkward turn at darts
and miss so badly even the Cyclops bulls-eye laughs at me
and I won't forgive you this because
it's the first time I have wanted to be different
and I won't forgive you for it …

…later when you think I'm sleeping I hear crying
and it stops me breathing for an instant
until, in the same way that winter's slow freeze seeps in,
I feel scar tissue forming across the wasteland of
how we hurt each other and it keeps spreading
until the grey thin light of early morning
when I climb down from my high horse
and despite myself I hold you
and despite yourself you want me to
and we go on with a few new wounds to tend to…

# God of the B-Sides

In a ground-floor hotel room she had
a polite nervous breakdown; she played
only the B-sides of it and in the glare
of the city she walked into night-time
and walked into morning and she slept
and slept and slept. She dreamed of boredom
of time-warps of white-sliced-pan lives and
dreary-era Paul Simon songs, always the B-Sides,
she squinted at relics she should have felt
something for and sang nationalist rants
with drunks in the working-man's bar on
the corner, she woke to broken glass and
impossible sunlight and she walked and
she walked and she walked past Sunday's
afternoon dancers, Stalinist statues, past murals
that seemed like cartoons and she met
urban fox foragers in alleys of trash-can nostalgia
who acted like she'd never existed and those days
she didn't so she gave her shoes to a tramp
who said may your god bless you whoever
he she or it is, and that made her start
crying in daylight out walking so she prayed
an atheist's prayer to the god of all B-sides
but he she or it didn't listen.

# Ghost

In November Connemara took a notion
to paint itself a gaudy European blue,
and flirt with cloud puffs
more often featured in children's crayon drawings
than in any actual sky.
It dressed its bog and foothills
in Chinese print shades
purples and faint mauves,
it laid cattle out to sleep mid-afternoon
as if they were at pasture in the Golden Vale
and down by the scrappy shoreline,
beside the rust-stained slatted shed
the parish graveyard hid
the fresh-dug bed of some young joyrider
who didn't think to emigrate.

# A Poem for My Son

Stop with your clicking, take your face
from the blue screen light's attractions and
head down, down to the street and kick football on it
take off your shirt and make goals with it
claim fouls win lose or draw it, be a sore loser then spit
on the future, lean on a corner wall while night falls,
pass twilight with people un-invented yet, watch everything
note it, then deal yourself in for the pleasure, your guys
your girls and their decadence, swim in your fear of each other
share yours with them, spend it, trip on shoelaces untied
stay heedless, get reckless, French-kiss someone
for the hell of it the look, the pose of it recoil slightly
from the feel of it, but grow a bit, welcome in the new gentleness
go off in cars driven by amateurs, time's moving too fast
and you're scared of it, that's half the joy of it
you there soaring, back-seating it, you aren't there yet
so submit yourself, go with it know some day
you'll be driving steering clear of the checkpoints in it
wear headphones everywhere and think for now and forever
that one song holds the key to existence; sing it
and mean it make sure you mean it but go on
go down, down on the street to it.

# Frontier Dogs

*for my inner conspiracy theorist*

Morning was a snarling fantasy
and the frontier dogs howling
were strangers, mongrels
you said there'd been an eclipse
and slipped off – you slithered
and I thought of lizards basking
and liked it, I wallowed
in your departure for centuries
then I froze up and it made
my mind sharper, I thought
you good-for-nothing
occult-sniffing bastard
look what you've done to us.

My breath plumed out
it vaporised and I orbited
until exhaust fumes rose up to me,
they listed thinned and drifted
and I was absorbed in them
I was merged into the pollution
of some imaginary city
I fell to earth then, I sank down to it
and I was part of a sea of peoples
walking toward some clamouring oblivion
it shone for us I walked towards the noise
towards the racket,
I chased after the lustre,
what else could I have done?
My tired feet beat out a tattoo
he's gone
he's gone
he's gone
but more strangely than anything
they kept walking
on and on and on.

# Death in Europe

on a hill top terrace
overlooking a ski slope
in the pretty Tyrol region of Austria
just outside Wörgl
(which, if you are interested
once had its own currency)
I ate cake, drank very good coffee
and watched a man and his missus
walk up the hill towards me
at the steps of the café
the man paused beside a tub full of flowers
someone had thoughtfully put there
and clutched at his chest,
he said something Austro-Hungarian
no more than one sentence,
then he died in a manner so civilised
his wife's tears seemed excessive
and the people trying to revive him
seemed like peripheral peasants
rummaging at their own lowly concerns,
I thought to offer his widow my chair
or the handkerchief I obviously
should have been carrying
but I was in that part of inevitable Europe
where I am not sure if death
is a cause for concern or for sentiment
so I went as scheduled, off to my conference
where I spoke eloquently
with civilised others
about something
many people died for
though obviously
none of us mentioned this.

# The Irish in Britain

Had I lived I would be fifteen now
scrawling your name on my copybook
as some listless teacher droned,
we made our own spells our own rules
you and I painted circle 'A's
on canvas bags with Tippex,
and later in my bedroom I would make
you sniff it so we could channel
some imagined high and discuss
all the things that anarchism isn't
those were the only times
you ever came close to barefaced
to some great reveal.

We sang Billy Bragg songs
and grasped at something bigger,
something we hoped we could fit in,
I held your hand while we marched
against apartheid as if it hadn't
anything to do with us but the sixth years
called you faggot and gave you
a lacklustre kicking even their own hearts
weren't in it, still and all
something in you sickened and we were lost
to ignorance and ecstasy
to the worst you had to offer to yourself
we were lost to poppers,
to the summers in London
you spent sucking off bricklayers:
desultorily fucking.

You came home at the dark end
of your glue and aerosol dream
with a starry plough tattoo, as if some
or other republic waited here for you
had I lived I'd be forty now
but comrade you were never
coming with me —
more's the pity.

# Creatures

Creatures, my promises weren't false
when I made them, when
I said I'd take care of you
I expected certain things from your behaviour
when I said you are good people
it meant I think I am better.
I thought you were all neutral
and that I could mould you but now
you snivel there at foot-level bleating
and wonder why I must ignore you;
well you're trying to be mirrors
and I am dodging those particular reflections
this was never my intention.

Creatures, I am sheepish and I hate it
I only meant to save you
like the daddy-long-legs whose
limbs I accidentally amputated on
a daring release-from-bathtub mission
that went a little sca-ways, like that
you're lying where you fell, defeated
and worse you are needy,
you weren't meant to raise objections,
I can't bear it, I must go now
and find myself
some others who need rescuing.

# The Morning After

Crack-limbed trees splay themselves at Coole
falling they tore the earth's flesh asunder
now lying everywhichway like battlefield corpses,
they leave great hunks of vacant sky brutalised.

The lake flows in angry ripples up pathways
it consumes the picnic tables, the shrubbery
it surrounds the ornamental cedars and
leaves them floating without foundations.

Further in the water gets oil-black and sinister
it laps at deep thickets the storm almost couldn't penetrate
where like victims re-encountering childhood traumas
the trees creak and find new fault lines.

Sometime in the future some sideways breeze
will claim them as trophies, they'll fall then
from wounds made this morning; from the violence
of newly-emptied spaces, from escaping.

# Safe House

*for Lisa, and for Colm whose house it was written in*

When I heard about you
I was in a house
full of love and was glad of it.

In the north wind
that week it was unthinkable
to think that the Gulf Stream
caressed us but it did
it held us in our safe houses
with our pets
with our family photos
with our currents of love.

When I heard about you
I was in a house
full of love and was glad of it,
I am glad there are safe houses
and underground railways
for runaways
for subversives
for the different
even if you
didn't find one in time.

# Cash for Gold

At twenty to three in the morning when I was already
reluctantly sober I happened to run into Fergal
who was standing morose and cold looking at some street corner
it had been years since I'd seen him so of course we got talking
and how badly he was doing reassured me,
isn't that something rotten?

Ferg said he suffers from his nerves now and he told me
he'd won four thousand on the ching-chings a month or so
before but that he was less lucky with the object of his affections
who upped and left him before he could tell her he'd booked them
in the Athlone Radisson for two nights bed and breakfast
just, like, for the hell of it and how in two days more he'd spent it
he blew the fuck out of it, it was brilliant he said
everyone should do it once but I suppose 'Caesar's'
or 'Claude's Casino' got the benefit as if we couldn't have
predicted that then this week he got double payment
from the social and he chucked it in the slots, it took him
all of twenty minutes during which he thought of nothing
he says it's a type of pureness going through money like that
but yesterday his rent was due and he pawned his Gibson
in the cash for gold and they gave him way less than its value
Gibsons are the best guitars of all he told me, and yeah
he'd already spent the money, in the morning he's going back in
because he sees no reason not to pawn his amp as well
sure what use is it? With no music coming through it?
He says there goes his chance of scoring a paying gig at Christmas
and he has nothing due to him till the Wednesday after next one
social welfare should never give him two weeks' money together.

When we were fourteen he was beautiful, the subject
of a thousand toilet cubicle love hearts, he was able to mimic
every hit song and play it to us we were certain he'd be famous
and we'd be mortals earth-stuck and suburban, but there's not
much method to this world's pecking order is there?
And in fairness having nowhere else I should be
at four in the morning except a cold and damp street corner
well I'm not in any position am I to think myself superior?

Back when we all hung around in bunches, Dan had got a car
and we took it on a kind of sordid teenage venture to the dump
at night-time where we wreaked havoc with a pellet gun
and a real-deal shot gun, we learned to shoot there, using
the rats as targets, we picked them off at random and got wild
with cordite and kickbacks to our shoulders, with yahoos
and 'look I got it' shouts, we got crazy with the guilt of it:
the wholly unaccustomed violence, but Fergal kept his back
to us and just sat there on the bumper smoking
he wouldn't even flick the headlights to illuminate our murders.
When we'd used up every last cartridge we went back to him
half scared and fully exhilarated and we piled in to the car
with all our bloodlust sated and in a hurry to get gone before
some fucker caught us but Ferg was crying and even though
we hugged him he never told us what was up, he sat there
in the back seat squashed and blubbering while we hit potholes
with the suspension and our buttocks suffering, gravel
from the bad roads flying skywards and Kenny said
it was because some fine beoir dumped him that he was crying
but I don't remember if Fergal ever answered that one.

Last night I shared my chips with him; we were reminiscing
and talking about being forty and how it overtook us,
he told me he's got a habit of borrowing money from a hard-chaw
even if he doesn't need it, because it gives him tension
fear takes over when he's frightened and owes a man
who'll beat him senseless and he forgets his heartbreak
and how he can't go in his bedsit since Rosemary left him
and I tried to console him by spouting clichés like 'Fergal man
if she hurts you she's not worth it' but he wouldn't listen
he just said he'd never understand money he just didn't get it
and that he wanted to ask me one question, and I said
'ask away man, sure if I can I'll answer' 'If something never hurt you'
he said 'how could you just kill it? The rats remember?
I never knew a girl could do that, just bang bang bang
and you were laughing at them' and I had to tell him
Fergal don't believe it, of all the species we are the most vicious.

He went off then, said his friend Katerina has been having
claustrophobic episodes in her Cedar Park Apartment
and because of it she sleeps in Newcastle now in the front porch
of the student residence and that sometimes when he can't sleep
he goes there to talk to her 'she's nice,' he said, 'do you want to
come with me?' I didn't, that fella's altogether too gentle,
but I won't say that sometimes I wasn't tempted
these days, not that much separates us.

# Scheme

somedays I am applicant,
somedays I am unsuccessful applicant,
or one of more than two hundred highly qualified applicants
most days now I am not disappointed by this
because I had to make some cuts
and first I severed the part where hope lives
yes that was severe but remember
we're all suffering here.
Last August when things were rawest
Pat who hasn't worked since the year the pope visited
told me that his best advice is to do a crossword
every day and walk the promenade from end to end,
three miles he says, that's what it takes
to keep you sane and keep your brain in shape.

I find myself that it's best to only ever
open e-mails or letters on a Wednesday
because then they won't upset the weekend
or write the week off from the get-go
just there, at the apex is when they can best be dealt with
on Wednesdays I can cope with all the dear-john, final-reminders
and we-thank-you-for-your-interest messages
by making sure I get another letter sent before Friday lands in
– that I make one more application.
Here's the secret though, I buy a lottery ticket too
and I leave it in my pocket, I don't even scratch it
and that means that I can have a ship waiting
out on the horizon about to come in,
for the whole weekend no one can say it isn't
and I can tell my friends in Tigh Neachtain's
yea this job's in Limerick
and I'm made to measure for it
no no I didn't hear back yet
but I'd expect at least an interview,
ah there are green shoots
the economy's picking up you know.

# This Poem is an Affair

It takes the odd weekend away claiming 'business'
shares foods it doesn't like with someone else for breakfast
it finds itself developing new interests in things it never before considered,
it checks its phone incessantly for messages then
re reads some of them over and over thinking it is being surreptitious
and that its new scents and poses are going unnoticed,
it plays a different station on the radio then doesn't listen,
is more attentive than is usual to the children
it thinks a little more highly of itself than it used
sucks in its guts then despairs of ever measuring up to
the decent poem it meant to be back when starting,
at this stage of its life it makes able use of language and structure
and says it sleeps *mostly* in the spare room these nights
its looks linger on the bare shoulder of its new beloved
as she's shepherded out for dinner without it
it doesn't flinch from holding the hand it took in marriage,
it takes that for granted (not seeing any need there to be overtly romantic)
just in case though, it makes certain she's not left craving anything carnal
man, this poem gets action,
in its early verses this poem could have been at risk
of something stupid and impulsive
but as the rhythm builds it slips into a formula where
instead of being an affront to tradition it becomes something
that inadvertently supports it.

# In Cill Rialaig Trying Not to Write 'Digging'

Hag-like I was hanging out on a cliff top
where I got sequestered in pre-Famine cottages,
I was sent here for poeting; 'stay there would you
and write something' the crew from Listowel said
but somehow I couldn't get down to it
so I read some Gramsci and thought about privilege
and artistry, whether words actually matter,
I ate some toast and looked out towards the sea
and the islands who don't bother with language
then I shook myself up from my dreaming
and blighted the landscape with lycra,
I ran down the hill from the village
trying to exercise myself and to not think
about patronage on the morning after the pardon
of the Magdalenes for their non-sins by our non-king.

I ran alongside glowering brown hillsides
and down below to my right the sea was catching
what shimmer it could from a tight winter sky
and at a low-sized bungalow with pines singing outside
and crows chanting like guard dogs at me a big man
stooped over at a turf stack
to fill his bucket with turf
and I thought of the nature of work
and then scoffed at myself, the nerve of me
and he went on with his chores,
he was wide-shouldered and tall
a man like a house old and all as he was
and he could fit several sods in each hand
if he wanted and it's funny that once
I could have married him or someone so like him
as to make little difference and I thought
I am supposed to be writing but I said a prayer
that I wouldn't go back to my cottage and write 'Digging'
I'd rather write nothing even if I concede
that it needed to be said once and fair play to Heaney

for doing it (and thanks to the women for the tea and the biscuits)
but is there any need for us to mimic it? Still
looking at turf stacks and thinking of writing –
in a way I was asking for it but I pray, I plead
to not be derivative, but it's futile isn't it?
it fills me with horror if I admit that I'm destined
to repeat the same cycle over and over
to think nothing new under the sun
and I know about Mahon who seems to conclude
that the only true poetry is to not write it
but he does anyway just not so very much
as he used to, on the way back I passed the postman
and made him a symbol of something
of structure and timekeeping and capitalism
and I thought I am a prisoner of theory and culture

and instead of making sermons from our ability to kiss
the hands of killers of children, which in fairness
is what our culture specialises in and I resolved to refuse it
to not tip my cap to it in future, as I ran up the last hill in a spurt
that I later regretted I resolved to explode it
instead of being subversive and half flirting with resistance
but still and all submissive, I promised that from now on
I'd outright confront things.
As I came around the home stretch
I saw a sign on the laneway that leads to the beach
and it read: Private No Trespassing! and in
the very same way as a private poem published
it has no means of telling the seaweed,
the fish, or the water who might come in and who mightn't
and I am definitely digging for something;
I just can't put my finger on it.

# Traffic

Yesterday surrounded by traffic and tribes of people going
about their business, to the hum of the engine, to the backdrop
of getting myself somewhere I was thinking of your generous mouth
of your hand, curled on my knee as I drove us, I was thinking
of your breath on my neck in the mornings of how gentle
and stubborn you were about rising; every soft curve of you
used to lie there resisting in a velvet revolt, I was thinking of you
with your back to me in the kitchen chopping tomatoes,
you need to watch what you're eating you'd say
and those meals were offerings I was thinking of your hand
on the small of my back in the hospital as we went to be there
for an old friend's departure and I was thinking how I only remember
fragments of what we said in all the hours we spent talking or
the things we did then, but I have this catalogue, a playlist of touches
that I can put on shuffle when I'm alone and driving in traffic.

# Hotel Poems

at the elevator door on floor eight
of the shrink-wrapped apart-hotel
(families and pets always welcome)
there's a thirteenish girl
and a puppy on a lead, waiting
they're plump and dark-haired –
an exactly matched pair
she says he's half lab-half alsatian,
I say isn't he lovely? And to please her
or to appease my need to touch something
that's not antiseptic in this place
I pet him and he squirms in delight
then urinates slightly, leaving a dribble
on the chemical carpet in this chemical corridor
that we pretend not to notice
as we duck in to the elevator
giggling like children conspiring.

At midnight from the corridor on floor eight
of the shrink-wrapped apart-hotel
(families and pets always welcome)
shouts come; shut the fuck up
you little shit a man's voice says
no you shut the fuck up a girl's voice says
and then with a certain integrity
that's otherwise missing here
a door violently slams,
heavy footsteps recede and sobs breathe
in through next door's thin walls
I turn over in my manicured bed
in the shrink-wrapped apart-hotel
(families and pets always welcome)
and hope that unhygienic puppies
are everywhere they're needed
for licking upset
teenage faces.

# On Black Sand Beaches

*for Aoibheann McCann*

There's black power graffiti
on a glaring white wall at the harbour
where two German octogenarians with skin like bog bodies
are holding hands on a love seat in the early morning sun,
we all drink Ethiopian coffee from the taxi driver's café
the only place that's open at this hour
and I look out to where blue water meets blue sky
and wonder if it's worse or better to be depressed
in this luminous weather,
in this absolute place
when my own interior terrifies me.

Elaine once told me she thinks that feminism
has mostly meant poorer women
clocking in to do the wealthy's work for them
and she might be generalising
but it's hard to argue
that there isn't something in it
here on this formerly African island
where the women mopping floors
and changing my bed sheets
always have darker skin than me.

I tell one of them not to bother,
not to work too hard, but she's Indonesian
and doesn't understand my Irish-accented Spanish
why should she? Embarrassed, I tip her
and she pockets the money
with a look that belittles me,
a look I deserved, mind, for pretending
that she has the choices here
this might be where privilege lives
what privilege is:
on days like this
I sicken myself.

Don't ask me what poverty means
I am long since bankrupt
but Aoibheann and I can lay waste to free rum and cokes

and eat as much limp food as we want
from an all-inclusive buffet
which someone else will clean up after
we can lie on black sand beaches
and swim in warmer than normal seas while
we turn our own skins a bit darker.

In Emma's Mexican Cantina
loud-ish Mancunians direct Filipino women
to cook frijoles and sour cream
for Caucasians and while we eat them
we don't think of how some of our genocidal relations
must have laid waste, must have decimated this place,
we eat our beans and don't wonder why Kanye West
hip-hopping it on the flat screen TV
in the corner is the only black person
we see here on this formerly African island.

Worst of all though is how last night
my subconscious betrayed me
and I dreamt that dark people swam towards me
that they came in poor clothes
perched on the prows of thin rickety boats
and they carried small children and bags of possessions
which they tried to keep out of the water
and that's what has me up this early,
in the dreams where these people came towards me
I wasn't out on the coast to welcome them in,
I wasn't gathering blankets or food for them
I wasn't throwing my fellow humans life-preservers
and helping them land, in my dream
I was manning the barricades
to stop them from coming and later,
much later, after failing to halt them
I was running away terrified,
and now I'm up early looking at black power graffiti
on a glaring white wall in the harbour
and I am wishing I could un-dream
these new things I know about me
and my ancestors who must for certain
have done or not done something.

# No Me Molestes Más

Before I knew you
Barcelona silenced me
eight million busy moving
or hanging out in cafés smoking
and all that going on without me —
I found it cleansing
now everyone that passes me
is not you
but could be.


The smell of last night's meat
from sweaty Argentinean restaurants
down in La Barceloneta molests me
before breakfast and the fish nets
in the doorways seem affected
until I see the leather skin
of the men who use them,
who spit their cigarette phlegm
in the early mornings
onto the sidewalks where
I am walking daylight into
my insomnia
without you.


Before I knew you
birds of prey hanging on thermals
above Montserrat
emptied out my innards
and left me weightless
that's just one
of many things
you've taken.

# Chevaux de Frise

I couldn't kiss you at the station in Valencia
your mouth was too hungry for me
I couldn't touch you in our attic room in Antwerp
because you felt like slippers, like suburbia —
like my unavoidable future, I couldn't sleep with you
in lace-edged Bed and Breakfasts in the Gaeltacht
with some Bean an Tí half-listening, by the sea
in Spiddal I couldn't so much as look at you directly
and at Dun Aengus I struggled with my own significance,
I felt too small to receive affection and I can tell you
the thin partitions and stained headboards
in our Paris bedroom didn't fix it, Mexico City shocked me
and I think if you were with me I would have held you
like an amulet, like magic, like you and me forever
but I don't think I can prove that here on the promenade
in Dun Laoghaire because I have to tell you:
I've never once felt anything for anyone in Dublin.

# I Am Not Tired

I'm with my tribe of greenish-pale people and I am not tired;
we're as far apart as we can be in this night-time lighthouse
that calls cars in like moths from the flyover,
here everyone's watching and everyone knows it – we're in this together
but there's no chance of talking that's not what the rules are,
sometimes the coffee's good and needed but mostly it bears
no relation to those beans in verdant greenish posters of far more
beautiful people eating things fairtraded in far-off places
that don't look anything like what we're eating or where
we're sitting, on our billboards there'd be a belly protruding
over a belt bought back in leaner times and make-up that looked
way better in the mirror before the jaded waitress left for work
there'd be faded confections on plates beside elbows, and watchstraps
that have no significance here where time's excommunicated
there'd be the chins of both sexes resting on palms and what of it?
We'd all look static and washed up but that's not how it is,
we're just insomniacs; late travellers, truck drivers,
cabin-fever-house-escapers and bereaved sons on their way to homes
that aren't theirs anymore, we are second thought lovers all greenish
and we're here because it's a place that has time excommunicated
and we are not tired, when I leave I'm exploring some territory
never previously navigated; it seems I'm hacking my way
to my own back door and it's greenish, as insipid as the lobby
of a two-star that in the brochures promised more and my tribe
are with me but they're shattered from not acting disappointed
and the old bloke's put his back out at the disco that he wished
he never went to, seriously he'd have settled for two pints in the local,
and a game of darts with the resident expert on everything
and here the bleary queen of peaks and troughs is splayed out
in the corner, she's so corpulent you'd think she'd never fit in the urn
she's had ready for years, be prepared she told me, but she doesn't have
spare tights though she always rips them and whatever it is with her
she isn't saying and why should she? The barman is polishing glasses
picked out by spotlights that never put their beam on
the mouldy drink soaked carpet and yeah this is England
or should I say Britain? I must be raving, but I'm queuing for the ferry

in a car that's someone else's, driving down to the underbelly
then sea-legging it around the decking where halogen has made us
all spectres with black pits for eyes and don't be fooled;
we like it like this, there's sea outside the window as remote
as a breast back in childhood but it doesn't stop the truckers wanting
to be mothered and then I'm spat out to the glamour of rigids and semis
and box vans past straight-edged warehouses with floodlights
and I am not tired, I pass a crime scene in the making;
two men in overalls by a side wall kick the skull of some prone figure.
I keep driving and wondering how we decided what constitutes beauty
the lights at the junction indicating something more friendly downtown
don't tempt me; it's off down the continent through swamps with ghosts
of white horses splashing and they're not half as pretty as how
the light hit the guy getting the kicking but it's night-time and I'm in it.
I light a cigarette, driving with my elbows, some Catholic radio station
is blaring in Spanish but this is France isn't it? Well it's a four-lane
where my car is smallest and there's a stand of pines, a rest-stop
and I'm driving through beer ads, a motel is all glaring and flat-roofed
low down from the motorway I don't stop though I'm propelled
– it's night-time and I am not tired; somewhere to the left
there must be mountains but all I can see are wipers lulling me
and a yellow fuel light on the dashboard then again a truck stop
is calling and I'm with my tribe, the greenish communion and we aren't tired
I sleep on the counter, head on my forearms and beer bottles
not coffee cups litter the lit tables of my comrades, it takes the four-lane
downhill sweep and a sheen of water off behind to remind me
that there isn't anyone with me, at daylight I pull in but I am not tired
just jealous of the glare's intrusion squinted heat through the windscreen
wakes me; I'm at my front door but it's insipid then I come to
and I'm all continental, raving, the Basque country hits me
like a language from nowhere and beside a surf beach I'm parked up
I'm crying, two days on and I am not tired but I'm reciting
mish-mash nursery rhymes and can't stop it, having come this far
I can report that I saw nothing thought nothing, met no one and I tried
to go further but all there was was the queen of laddered legs ahead
and behind my front door – all greenish, and I still am not tired.

# Excuse No. 114 (Intimacy Avoidance Section)

Without even making much of a fizz about it
I dissolve in water when submerged, in my schooldays
understandably, I avoided swimming practice and got myself
a name for evasive action that has stuck with me till now,
in adolescence I didn't drive fast or drink young, I was different;
for my kicks I had only to stand on the shoreline and
as unpredictable waves rolled within a whisker of my feet
I could surf on the adrenalin of nearly disappearing,
now as an adult, like privileged Victorian-era lords and ladies
I stay indoors when it's raining, I find even light drizzle
makes me vaguer and makes the streetscapes blurry
and though I have a car I either drive it dirty or get someone else
to wash it because my worst nightmares are composed of
its sunroof leaking as the crazy swirling car-wash brushes
pass overhead, I am as yet uncertain whether water
is the only liquid that has such a strong effect on me,
so you shouldn't take it personally if I refuse to kiss you;
if you are one of those lovers who does it particularly wetly,
you'll understand that one kiss could be the end of me.

# On the Tear

The paired and single girls click-clicking home
on their Sunday morning walks of shame don't see me
and two boys with quiffs and a whiff of something expensive
giggle past me shaking their asses like ganders
and I am an old laying hen. My cigarette won't light
so I throw it away and discover that it was the last one,
the cigarette box is desolate and I curse the last fag in the world
I scrabble after it but it's gone like others before it down, down
the Corrib and off to the sea there'll be no search mounted
no divers, no helicopters, it's me alone who must keen for it,
I sit back down from my knees and remember that somehow
during precedings I cut my feet on something,
I can't bring myself to look at them I throw back my head instead
and wonder if the river reflects the sky on its surface
why the sky doesn't reciprocate? If I went up to Eyre Square
I know I'd find a few fair-weather friends there but there's nothing
they'd give you without charging, they wouldn't give you
the steam of their piss so they wouldn't, they wouldn't reciprocate
if you see what I'm saying and I don't know where my shoes are,
the cars are all starting to wake up and go someplace,
they are leaving me, the cars are much-obliging people
who have to go somewhere and I'm on the canal bank
underneath eye-in-the-sky cameras feeling no danger,
I know the lads in at Mill Street can look down from the streetlights
and see me and the cars turning from Claddagh have their indicators
pointing at me; there she is, there she is they say, they wink at me
and I am an old laying hen who doesn't wink back,
and I'm drunk in public, I am a duck with no ducklings,
I am drunk in the morning and I have nowhere to go to get sober
so if I want to I'll sit on the corner and cluck to myself
while I wait for the morning to warm me.

# Some Thoughts On the Prospect of Internet Dating During the Future Which is Taking Place, Despite Itself, Just a Few Short Years After Our Break Up

I'll go through the profile photos and see
if I can spot anyone with uneven biceps showing
in their selfies, I'll make bets with myself:
if it's the left one I'll message them, if it's the right,
I'll go on, I'll go on as well I might, like a kite with no string,
when I narrow it down I'll choose a woman who keeps
her marmalade mind in a jar with a lid that you
could open for me without even trying and I'll choose a man
with petals for eyelids and a blink that brings bees out
from their hives, I know you'll like him and how I am with him
if he'll agree to come with me, and if he won't I'll go for
whoever is willing to risk it and I'll be all things to all people
on our very first meeting, I'll be the best tapas you
or they've ever had in a bar with plastic tables
and tetra pack wine or I'll choose a place to meet up in where
books may or may not have been written or read by people like us
I'll choose a place like a fig with sweet gritty innards
that my dates and I can sit in not thinking,
I'll choose a place where someone once heard
the exact words they needed in that exact moment
and I'll be the one saying them and I'll be the one listening
as soft sounds drift in from the kitchen, I'll think of foodstuffs
and humans and touching without any hunger
because you won't be with me, I'll pay the bill out of guilt
or shame or loss or something – I won't feel what it costs me
and I'll set off walking through air thick-full of nothing
I'm a wheel with no axle, god love me, I still desperately
miss you and you're not in any of these pictures.

SARAH CLANCY is a page and performance poet from Galway. Her two previous collections are *Stacey and the Mechanical Bull* (Lapwing Press, Belfast, 2011) and *Thanks for Nothing, Hippies* (Salmon Poetry, 2012). Along with fellow Galway poet Elaine Feeney she released a poetry CD called *Cinderella Backwards* in 2013. She has been placed or shortlisted in several of Ireland's most prestigious written poetry competitions including The Ballymaloe International Poetry Prize, The Patrick Kavanagh Award and The Listowel Collection of Poetry Competition. In performance poetry Sarah has won the Cúirt International Festival of Literature Grand Slam Championships and has twice been runner-up in the North Beach Nights Grand Slam. In 2013 on her second go at representing Connaught in the All- Ireland Grand Slam Championships she was runner up. She has recently stopped sulking about this. In 2013 she received an individual artist's bursary from Galway City Council. She is frequently invited to read her work at various festivals and events around Ireland and abroad and can't believe she's still getting away with it. She is on twitter @sarahmaintains and can be contacted by e-mail at sarahclancygalway@gmail.com